CLASSICAL SOLOS FOR OBOE

15 Easy Solos for Contest and Performance
Arranged by Philip Sparke

ONLINE MEDIA INCLUDED
Audio Recordings
Printable Piano Accompaniments

PLAYBACK+
Speed • Pitch • Balance • Loop

To access recordings and PDF accompaniments visit:
www.halleonard.com/mylibrary

Enter Code
1526-5375-4101-3110

ISBN 978-1-70516-692-5

Visit Hal Leonard Online at
www.halleonard.com

World headquarters, contact:
Hal Leonard
7777 West Bluemound Road
Milwaukee, WI 53213
Email: info@halleonard.com

In Europe, contact:
Hal Leonard Europe Limited
1 Red Place
London, W1K 6PL
Email: info@halleonardeurope.com

In Australia, contact:
Hal Leonard Australia Pty. Ltd.
4 Lentara Court
Cheltenham, Victoria, 3192 Australia
Email: info@halleonard.com.au

WALTZ

MORITZ VOGEL
Arranged by PHILIP SPARKE

OBOE

CHORALE

Now praise, my soul, the Lord

JOHANN SEBASTIAN BACH
Arranged by PHILIP SPARKE

OBOE

00870090

HUMMING SONG

from *Album for the Young*

ROBERT SCHUMANN
Arranged by PHILIP SPARKE

OBOE

Moderato (♩ = 94)

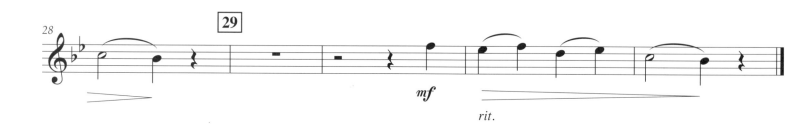

GYMNOPÉDIE NO. 1

ERIK SATIE
Arranged by PHILIP SPARKE

OBOE

Andante (♩ = 96)

Small notes opt.

rit.

00870090

5

I'M CALLED LITTLE BUTTERCUP

from *HMS Pinafore*

SIR ARTHUR SULLIVAN
Arranged by PHILIP SPARKE

OBOE

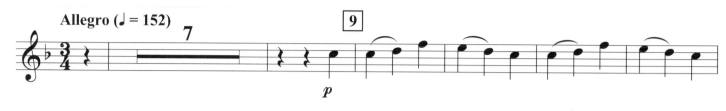

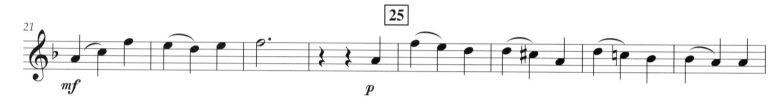

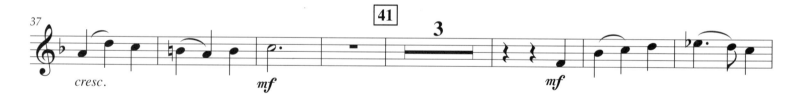

STUDY
Op. 37, No. 3

HENRY LEMOINE
Arranged by PHILIP SPARKE

OBOE

MINUET
(Z. 649)

OBOE

HENRY PURCELL
Arranged by PHILIP SPARKE

THEME AND VARIATION

from *Sonatina No. 3*

THOMAS ATTWOOD
Arranged by PHILIP SPARKE

OBOE

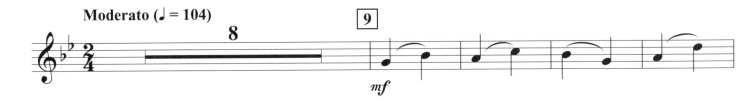

00870090

NORTHERN SONG

from *Album for the Young*

ROBERT SCHUMANN
Arranged by PHILIP SPARKE

OBOE

Moderato (♩ = 94)

TWO GERMAN DANCES

from *Twelve German Dances, D. 420*

FRANZ SCHUBERT
Arranged by PHILIP SPARKE

OBOE

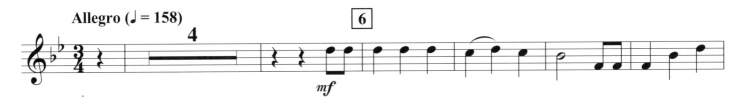

WATCH MAN'S SONG

from *Lyric Pieces, Op. 12*

EDVARD GRIEG
Arranged by PHILIP SPARKE

OBOE

GAVOTTE

JAN LADISLAV DUSSEK
Arranged by PHILIP SPARKE

OBOE

VIEN QUÀ, DORINA BELLA

OBOE

ANTONIO BIANCHI
Transcribed by **C. M. von WEBER**
Arranged by PHILIP SPARKE

Moderato (♩ = 96)

MINUET

from *Notebook for Anna Magdalena Bach*

Attributed to **CHRISTIAN PETZOLD**
Arranged by PHILIP SPARKE

OBOE

00870090

THE PRINCE OF DENMARK'S MARCH

from *Choice Lessons for the Harpsichord or Spinet*

JEREMIAH CLARKE
Arranged by PHILIP SPARKE

OBOE

(2nd time only)

rit.